The Day That Started Without Me

The Day That Started Without Me

Sumer Bibbs

LitPrime Solutions
21250 Hawthorne Blvd
Suite 500, Torrance, CA 90503
www.litprime.com
Phone: 1-800-981-9893

Published by LitPrime Solutions   05/04/2022

ISBN: 978-1-955944-77-9(sc)
ISBN: 978-1-955944-78-6(e)

Library of Congress Control Number: 2022905378

Contents

Introduction

This book is not a work of fiction; every word is true. This is the true story of a boy who grew up in a small town and had many hair-raising moments in his life that made his heart skip a beat. I'm sure that you will enjoy reading some of the humorous details of my early days.

I pray that as you read this book you will see what the Lord can and will do. This book is intended to increase your faith in the Lord so you can walk by faith and not by sight.

Many things occur in our lives; but when things happen that the doctors can't understand—when they can't see any chance of a patient surviving—that's the time that the Lord moves in and reveals his true power.

The reason I can say this without any hesitation is that I have experienced his power and have been inspired to share what the Lord has done in my life. What the Lord has done for me, he can do for you.

In this book I will also share some of the things that happened during my childhood and my adulthood. As you read this book you will understand why I titled it *The Day that Started Without Me*. I am sure that there has been or will be a day that starts without you.

Acknowledgments

I would like to dedicate this book to my loving mother and father who were two of the most wonderful people that ever lived. Although they both are gone, they will never be forgotten. I would also like to dedicate this book to my lovely wife, my three children, nine grandchildren, and my wonderful mother-in-law.

This book is also dedicated to my brother and to my two sisters and their families and to all my friends and relatives.

Finally, I pray that after reading this book, you will feel the same inspiration that I felt in writing it.

Chapter 1

How It All Began

I was born about fifteen miles from where I now live, in a small settlement where few people lived. I am sure Daddy was so proud that his first child was a boy. A few years later there was another boy born and then another boy; and finally Momma got her wish, for she had two girls.

Daddy took me back to this place some years back, and the old house that I was born in still stood. Although tattered and torn, it was still standing. Daddy said we stayed in that old house until Momma was able to move out, and then we moved to the city where we now live.

The first house I remember living in was near a funeral home. My friends would play with me until it got dark, and then they would vanish. We only lived there for a short while, and then Momma and Daddy bought their own place.

While we were still living near the funeral home,

my mother was changing my brother's diaper one day when he reached over and grabbed the open safety pin and swallowed it. Momma screamed and tried to shake the pin out with no success. There was a hospital within walking distance, so Momma grabbed my brother, told me to watch the house, and took off with my brother dangling in her arms.

Daddy finally made it home and asked in a rage where Momma was. I told him, and he took off for the hospital. After many hours they returned and said they had to take him to another hospital where the doctors would perform surgery. Momma and Daddy explained how the doctor had tried unsuccessfully to use magnets and long tools to get the pin out. After several days my brother was brought home. He had had surgery to remove the pin. From that day on, Momma would call me when she changed his diaper and would ask me to hold the pins until she needed them.

After some years we moved into our new place, and we really loved it. There were plenty of children there to play with, and we could play outside at night for there was no funeral home nearby. My brothers and I fought all the time. We broke the couch legs and the legs of Momma's sewing machine. The coffee table and end table had bricks under them for legs. There were broken doors and window panes too. We would fight over anything.

Every day when Momma and Daddy came home, we could look forward to getting whippings. When Daddy would start to whip us—or even before he had touched us—the crying would start. A lady lived across the street from us, and she would come and tell Daddy that he was going to kill us. Daddy would tell her that we were his chaps, and by then he would be really mad. There were times that I would see her coming and say to myself, "Please go away!" But she never did.

In our new neighborhood there were people who were always in everyone else's business. Neighborhood watch was in effect way back then, for there wasn't anything that you did that someone didn't see. Every mother in the neighborhood had the authority to correct you with any means necessary when you got out of place.

The old lady who lived across the street always wanted us to do something for her—go to the store for her, scratch her dandruff-infested head, be her maids and clean her house. Sometimes we would mow her yard. But no matter what we did for her, she would give us fifty cents. Back then fifty cents went a long way at the little corner store.

The lady who ran the little corner store would never wash her hands when we would go there. But we could get ten cookies from the big plastic jar for a dime and then get a big orange crush pop for six cents and have a meal. Sometimes I would get one of those big cinnamon rolls filled with raisins and a big root beer, and that would just about fill me up.

When Momma called us to eat after one of our trips to the store, we would already be full of junk food. Momma would get angry because she thought we had eaten at someone else's home. She would always warn us not to eat at other folk's houses and to come home when our friends were called to eat.

Chapter 2

About Our Town

The town that I grew up in was a small town with a population of around 5,600. The town had many things going for it. The Illinois Central Railroad ran through it, and it was so exciting as a small boy to go to the depot and watch the trains as they came in and people got off and others got on board. The conductor would shout out, "All aboard!" The big engine would rev up, and the train would slowly begin to move.

There were several small factories in our town that provided many jobs, and many people were employed at the tree nursery too. There were several cotton gins; there was a gristmill where people brought corn to be ground to meal, and the owner kept a third of the meal for his fee.

Daddy worked at the town's ice plant, and every chance I had I would go there so that I could watch the huge blocks of ice come out and watch him cut the large blocks into small blocks that he delivered to those who were not fortunate enough to have refrigerators yet. Daddy took these blocks of ice and placed them in iceboxes, which would keep the ice frozen for many days.

There were also several cafes in our town. Blacks weren't allowed to enter the front doors, though; we could only use the back doors. There were several drive-ins where we could drive up and place our orders. At the doctor's offices in town, we blacks faced signs that said "Colored" and "White only." Blacks would sometimes have to go to the doctor's office early to register and then go back home and wait. We would come back later that day, and still all the whites would get waited on first. In our town we were always met with signs that said "Colored" and "White only." I sometimes noticed whites walk by drinking fountains labeled "Colored" and spit in them.

The Trailways bus also ran through our town. Sometimes we were allowed to ride the bus but were ordered to go all the way to the back. I truly liked being in the back, for it was quiet since we were told to be quiet while riding. At the theater we blacks had to sit in the balcony to watch the movies, but that was good because we didn't have to worry about getting anything thrown on us. On some occasions, though, a black person would throw something down on the whites, and that would start a mess.

Chapter 3

My School Days

In our small town there were two schools: one for blacks only and the other for whites only. A few months after the law was passed that required schools to integrate, the school was burned to the ground, and with it went so many memories. Sadly the school was never rebuilt due to lack of funds, and the only choice we had then was to attend the white school. It was apparent that they didn't want us there, and really we didn't want to be there either.

Without a school of our own, we were sent to various places to be taught. Some of us went to churches where they had set up classrooms, and some went to classrooms created in the gym, which was still standing after the fire. Some went to other towns to go to school, and some even went to other states!

My school days were dreadful days. The older I got, the harder it was to remain in school. I had failed a couple of times, and all my friends had left me behind; so I lost all interest in school.

The streets in our hometown were always dirt and gravel; it was apparent that the asphalt always ran out just before it got to us. There weren't streetlights on most of our streets, so we lived dark, secluded lives. As children we loved to play games in the dark and do things that we weren't supposed to be doing. There wasn't much to do back then, but we found ways to make things happen. We would ride old broom handles that we called our horses, and we rolled old car tires up and down the streets.

My brother almost always wanted to be a mechanic, and it turned out that he was a good one. I remember one day, when he was working on Daddy's old car, he asked me to hold down the clutch while he tried to start the car from under the hood. As he worked on it, the old car started, and he yelled for me to get off the clutch. I did, but as I started to get out of the car, it took off backward and ran right through the newly installed cyclone fence next door, where the meanest woman in the world lived. All the noise brought her to her front door, and she laid down a cursing that brought Daddy out of the house. Oh, what a mess we were in! We stayed in trouble.

On Saturday night, Momma and Daddy would take us to town with them, and Daddy would park the car in front of a furniture store that had a color TV playing in the window. We would sit and watch TV while they shopped. My two brothers and I would argue about who would be the rifleman that night, but when the show got good and the rifleman went into action, it didn't matter anymore.

After we made it back home, Momma would began to unpack her groceries. Back then each package of wieners contained a prize, so there we would go again— one prize and three boys doesn't add up. So Momma would have to get involved to settle the matter.

On Sundays Momma would make us get ready for church, and after church Daddy would take us riding in the back of his old truck. I would always ride on the side that Daddy was on. He chewed tobacco, and when he spit, I would be right in the way. I finally realized that I was sitting on the wrong side!

There were several shoe stores in our little town, but we never had the chance to wear shoes from them. Daddy would take us to the nearby town where the man that he worked for had family members who ran a used shoe store. We would try on shoe after shoe until we each found a pair that felt comfortable on, and Daddy would buy them. After we had worn them a few times, the front ends would open like a mouth at the soles, and Daddy would say that we didn't take care of them. They would take us back later and get us replacement pairs that would last a few months.

The jeans and overalls that we wore were faded and had patches everywhere. We would kneel to play marbles and keep the knees worn out; and the backsides were often patched, for we were always climbing on things and getting hung on others.

Back in those days, I had many so-called friends, but as the years passed and we grew older, I found that

I only had one true friend. His name was Johnny, and we had many things in common. Johnny and I, as well as a few others, including some older guys, worked after school at a commercial laundry. Our job there was separating the white linens from the colored linens. There were sometimes white aprons that came in with flour on them, and every now and then one of the older guys would throw an apron and hit someone in the face with it. Everyone thought it was so funny except the one who had been hit; he would have so much flour all over his face that you could only see his eyes.

Most of the time it was late when we got off work, and Johnny would call his dad to come and get us. I will never forget Johnny's dad. He was a big, tall man, and he had a '57 Ford two-door hardtop that he drove with a lead foot. The thing that amazed me was that whenever he got to the place where he was supposed to turn, he would always seem to have passed it, until all of a sudden, he would turn the steering wheel hard. The tires would squeal, and we all would slide from one side of the car to the other. None of us had the nerve to say anything about his driving, though, for he already appeared to be mad at us for having to get up that late to come and get us. The ride home was short, but I was always glad when I got out of his car. Riding with Johnny's dad is when I truly learned to pray.

Chapter 4

Let's Go to
Grandma's House

When we kids heard the words "Y'all get ready! We are going to Grandma's house," joy filled our hearts because we knew that all our cousins would be there and we would have a good time.

It seemed that on the weekends everyone had the same plan: dump the children on Grandma. And Grandma never complained, for there was so much that she could find for us to do.

In the mornings when we got out of bed, the first words out of Grandma's mouth were, "Y'all go brush your teeth and wash your faces." One wash pan was filled with water, and usually it was cold. We all washed with the same water and dried our faces with the same towel. Down by the well, there was a dipper hanging on a nail that everyone used to drink water, and no one grumbled or complained. At bath time we would go outside and drag in the old, long tin tub that had been sitting in the sun all day so the water could be warm, and we all used the same water to bathe.

There was one thing at Grandma's house that I was truly afraid of: the old, nasty outside toilet. I was always small in stature, and each time I used it, I felt like I would fall through the hole on the seat. At night we were afraid to go outside, so we used a slop jar. In the morning no one wanted to take it out to empty it.

I have always had an inquiring mind, so I would watch Grandma while she worked and ask her questions. Once when I saw her with a board, rubbing clothes, I asked her what she was doing. She told me that the board was a rub board. She rubbed and rubbed to wash clothes using a hunk of lye soap that she had made from old lard and ashes from the fireplace.

On Saturday mornings before we all scattered, it was chicken-killing time. Grandma would first set up the black pot; and we would get water to fill it and then get dry wood to start a fire around the pot. Grandma would give us two pieces of wire with a hook on one end and some table scraps, and she would call the chickens. As they ate the scraps scattered on the ground, we would hook one chicken's leg with the wire and then grab it. Then Grandma would come, and we would take the other piece of wire to hold the chicken's head while she told one of us to hold the chicken's feet. Then Grandma would take an axe and cut the chicken's head off. It would jump up and down for a while before it died, and then Grandma would take the chicken to the pot of hot water and dip it up and down for while. After that she would lay it on a piece of tin and show some of us how to pick the feathers off, while the other kids were getting another one ready. Sometimes she would kill four chickens; she would fix two for dinner and use the other two to make dumplings for supper.

While we were at Grandma's house, there was something for everyone to do. If you weren't in the chicken killing, you had to make sure that there was stove wood for cooking and that there was water in the kitchen. On hog-killing days I really didn't want to go to Grandma's house because those days were always cold. But when we got there, it wasn't as bad as it seemed because all the neighbors would come and join in the hog killing and to help with preparing the hog. No one came looking to take anything home; they just came to help. Often they were offered some of the meat, but they would refuse; it wasn't like it is now.

There was only one part of the hog that they threw away: the hairs. They would save the hoofs to make hog hoof tea when we came down with colds. The head and feet would be boiled in the big black pot, and the women would make souse with it. Some of the women would take the intestines and clean them to make chitterlings. All the trimmings were used to make sausage and hams; shoulders and sides were salted down until they dried and then they were smoked.

The other time that I didn't want to go to Grandma's house was farming time. See, I never could use a hoe or pick a hundred pounds of cotton, so my job was go to the well and keep water for those in the fields. There were other things I never learned to do also, like milking cows. Even though I tried hard, I just couldn't get the milk to come out right. I was afraid of the cows, and I think the cows knew it.

After our chores were over, Grandma would tell us we could go play until mealtime. When it was time to eat, she would ring the dinner bell, and we would come running from wherever we were.

I had a cousin, just like that one particular cousin everyone else had, who knew *everything*; no matter what came up, he knew all about it. He introduced us to rabbit tobacco and showed us how to use old brown bags to make the paper to roll the cigarettes with. We would all sit in the woods, smoking like trains. After he introduced us to smoking, we started stealing Grandpa's Prince Albert tobacco when he was drunk. He also got my brother, who was a bed wetter, to eat the red berries of a polk salad plant by telling him they would stop him from wetting the bed. I found out later that those berries were actually poisonous. My cousin had been right: Those berries would have stopped my brother from wetting the bed. Really, they would have stopped him from wetting at all.

Our playing was rough and rugged. We climbed trees and rode limbs down. We cut Muscatine vines near creeks and ditches and would swing across while playing Tarzan and then drop down into ditches that were infested with snakes. There was no fear then. None of us could swim at that time, but the Lord was good then just like he is now, so none of us drowned when playing in the water.

There were holes in the floors of Grandma's house where the pine knots had fallen out, and through those holes you could see the chickens sitting on their nests. When they were off their nests, we would go under the house and gather the eggs. There were also cats and dogs that had made their homes under the house. I recall a time when one of my cousins looked through one of the holes and said that a cat was looking up at him. He went and got some melted grease from the stove and poured it into the cat's eyes, and you could hear the cat running and meowing under the house. Grandma began screaming, "What is wrong with that cat?" But nobody knew a thing. A few days later the cat was on the porch, and Grandma asked why the cat's face was so greasy. No one knew the answer to that one either.

Oh yes, there was a grandpa too. He was a man of very few words, but when he spoke, it was like E. F. Hutton had spoken. He never did too much; mostly all he did was give orders, and he made homebrew beer that he shared with his friends. On Saturday nights all his friends would come over and bring their instruments— fiddles, jugs, guitars, and harmonicas. Grandpa would get his jugs of homebrew and the glasses, and they would drink a while and play their instruments a while.

As they drank, they would begin to try to sing; they sounded like a record playing at the wrong speed. They also had the nerve to try dancing. Can you imagine a bunch of drunk men dancing? They looked like ants had gotten into their pants and they were trying to shake them out. We had figured out that Grandpa kept the raisins that he made the homebrew out of in the old trunk at the foot of his bed, and we had also discovered that we could take the pins out of the hinges and get to the raisins that way; so while he and his friends were playing and singing and dancing, we would get into his trunk. Grandpa finally found out what we were doing, but he didn't say a word.

One night Grandpa told us to go to bed early, but we couldn't figure out why. As soon as we got our clothes off, the door swung open and in stepped Grandpa with five switches in his hand. He put a chair in front of the door and laid four of the switches on it, holding the chair with his other hand. He asked who wanted to be first, and of course no one volunteered. He said that since no one would come forward, he would pick one of us, and he did. The whole time that he was whipping us, he reminded us that he hated a thief and told us that if we stole again he would kill us. I stayed away, trying to be last; I thought that he would be too tired to whip hard when he got to me—but I was so wrong. It seemed that he had just gotten warmed up when my turn came.

Also in that old trunk, Grandma kept Hershey candy bars. My cousin would steal some of her candy bars and share with us. Grandma found out that someone had been stealing her candy, but, like Grandpa, she never said anything. When Grandpa went to town, he bought Grandma a large pack of Ex-Lax. She removed the Hershey bar from the trunk, ate it, and put the Ex-Lax in its place. The next time my cousin went into the trunk, he didn't share with us. He ate the whole pack of Ex-Lax himself, thinking he was eating candy, but oh, what a surprise he had!

Grandma called us together and told us what she had done and said that the person who had taken her candy would start running after awhile. Sure enough, while she was talking, my cousin took off for the toilet down the hill, but he didn't make it. Back then we all wore one-piece cotton garments called unions. Each one had a little door at the back that was kept closed with buttons; but after my cousin's episode with the ex-lax, there were no more buttons on his unions. He tore them all off in his hurry to relieve himself. For several days he couldn't make it to the toilet in time. No one wanted to sleep with him for fear he might have an accident; we didn't even want to be around him. So he made a pallet on the floor and learned how to wash and hang clothes on the line too.

Grandma finally felt sorry for him and fixed him some kind of tonic to help him out of his misery. Finally, he came to Grandma and admitted that he had stolen her candy. Grandma told him there was never any doubt that he had done it. She laughed and asked him if he would do it again, and he hastily said, "No, ma'am."

Grandpa had an old '52 Ford pickup truck, and the only smooth spot on it was inside the truck bed. There were trees standing along the road to the house, and when Grandpa went to town, you could hear him on his way back home, for every tree that stood along the road got a lick as Grandpa drove by. I have yet to figure out how he made it home; his eyes were almost closed due to his homebrew drinking, but he made it.

Grandma's house was cold in the winter and hot in the summer. In the winter we would pack rags under doors and around windows to try to keep the cold air out. There were so many quilts and blankets on our beds that we couldn't move and we would eventually get out of bed so that we could finally rest after a long night of wrestling with all the covers Grandma had laid down. Before we went to bed we would stand before the fireplace to get hot on one side, and then we would turn to heat our other sides. Our clothes would get to smoking, and someone might grab your leg and burn you while you stood there. We would also take a quilt and hold it near the fireplace until it got warm and then run with it and jump into a warm, cozy bed.

My brother was a bed wetter, and he would wet his side of the bed while we slept and then try pushing someone else onto his wet spot while he or she slept. Sometimes it worked, but sometimes the cold, wet spot woke the person up before my brother had moved him or her.

Chapter 5

My Other Grandma's House

Like everyone else, I had two grandmas, and the one that I will describe in this chapter is the one that we didn't spend much time with, which I truly regret. My grandparents on this side were more serious, which means they didn't play. I do have a few memories of them, though.

Once my brothers and I were playing in their car and somehow knocked the car out of gear. At the time they lived on a hill, and there was a well at the edge of the hill. As the car sped backward down the hill, it leveled the well, and we got a whipping like you would never believe. But all in all, I truly loved my grandparents.

Chapter 6

In Our Neighborhood

In our hometown everyone seemed to love everyone else, and anyone could correct us kids when we were wrong. Neighbors would share whatever they had. Often you would see a child going to the house next door with an empty vessel and then returning home with the vessel full; in a few days you would see that same child going back to the neighbor's house with the same vessel—only this time the vessel would be full as he returned what his mother had borrowed.

I have always had an inquiring mind, and I observed many things during my childhood that amazed me. One of those things was seeing the old mothers going to white ladies' houses to work from sunup to sundown. They would drag home bundles of old newspapers in one arm and in the other carry vessels that contained leftover meals. These women would take the leftover meals and feed them to their families; they would use the newspapers to plaster the walls in their homes, for they didn't live in brick houses but in shacks that had cracks everywhere.

These ladies would combine flour and water and boil the mixture to make a glue to plaster their walls with the newspapers to keep their families warm. Some of the paper was packed around the windows and doors to keep the cold air out. The remainder of the newspaper was used to start fires around the large black pots that they used to boil their cloth. One of the strangest things that I ever saw was a grandma putting a blue liquid in a big black pot filled with boiling water. She put her white clothes into that blue water and poked at them for a while, and then later, when she took them out, rinsed them, and hung them on the clothesline, they were so white they could nearly blind you.

Even in small, quiet towns, things do happen sometimes that draw everyone closer for a while; and then as time passes, the old lifestyle resumes.

Chapter 7

This Is For Our Mother

There was a lady in our lives that my brothers and sisters grew very fond of—our mother.

I remember Momma would always get up early in the morning to prepare breakfast, and Daddy would shout out, "Alright, y'all, jar the floor!" We knew he meant get out of bed, and while we washed our faces and brushed our teeth we could hear Momma passing gas. One of my brothers would say, "Ohhh, Momma," and she would start to laugh. She would laugh so hard that she sounded like a motorcycle starting up. She was the one that taught my two brothers, my two sisters, and I how to pray; she taught us how to say thank you when someone gave us something or did something for us. It was our mother who taught us about Jesus—who he was and what he meant to her and what he should mean to us.

She taught us how to read and how to spell and how to do arithmetic. There was much she didn't know, but what she knew she was willing to share with us and with others. No matter what tasks she had set before her for the day, she always made sure that a meal was prepared before she did anything. Mother always worked outside the home, and most of the time she would have dinner started early. She depended on me to finish cooking it since I was the oldest child, and I did.

Mother was a seamstress in her own way, and she would make our shirts and pretty little dresses for my sisters. My shirts looked good to me until I wore them to school and the children made fun of me. There was a fight over it.

I remember how Mother made lye soap with old grease and Merry War lye. I can see her now with that old black pot with that paddle she had made, stirring that concoction. She would put it out to dry, and then she would cut it into blocks. She washed our clothes with it in an old wringer-type washer, and when she finished washing, she would save some of the wash water in a tin tub to use as our bath water.

There was also something that my mother did that I still don't understand: eat dirt. She would send us to a certain dirt bank to get her some dirt, and she would literally eat the dirt.

Momma had a sock with a large amount of money in it, and she carried it with her, pinned to her underwear. One day while visiting the hospital, she lost it, and somehow someone called her and returned the money to her. Unfortunately, during her illness later on, we forgot the money she kept hidden, so someone at the hospital got it.

Mother also taught us to love one another and to love others even if they didn't love us back. Momma was a very happy person. Throughout her life she never complained. She would always joke about things; even on her deathbed she found a way to smile and joke. As Momma's condition worsened, she became weaker and weaker, and the pains grew more severe. Finally one day the Lord saw that she had suffered enough. He called her name and told her to come on home, and she slowly slipped away from us.

I truly thought that I was stronger than I was, for I was giving my younger siblings comfort and encouragement; but at the funeral, when it came time for me to view Momma's body, I never made it to the casket. I fainted and was carried out. Losing Momma was unlike anything else that I've ever experienced in my life. There is no one and nothing that can ever take the place of a mother. Although years have passed, the thought of not having her here is still sometimes unbearable.

Some Saturday nights Momma and Daddy would go out to the club. They would buy us some kind of toy that we would play with in the car while they sat in the nightclub. We could hear the blues playing on the machine, and every so often Momma would come to the car to check on us.

Mother made sure that we got up on Sundays and got ready for church. She would take us even though we sometimes didn't want to go, but she never knew that. Every Sunday after church we would always go visiting; and it seemed like wherever we went we were expected, for there was always plenty of food prepared. Once we were visiting an aunt's home for dinner, and the food was really good. As I ate, I began to hum a tune, and Daddy told me to stop. I did stop, but I soon started back up again. This time Daddy didn't say a word. All he did was take his powerful hand and slap me from the table.

Chapter 8

This Is for Our Daddy

My daddy wasn't the friendliest person I knew, especially to us. He would take his fist and maul my head with it and tell me that I was going to learn or else. I never did and didn't want to know what the "else" was. He had me so afraid of him that I often had flashbacks of his treatment of me. There were nights that we spent with our grandparents when someone would try to wake me and I would begin reciting my multiplication tables.

I worked hard trying to satisfy Daddy, but I always fell short of his expectations. He would take us fishing and tell us to be quiet or he wouldn't take us fishing again. He told us to wait until our corks went under before we pulled up our lines. Sometimes a fish would be on one of our lines, just running with it, but we wouldn't say anything because we were trying to stay quiet and wait on the cork. Daddy would see it and shout out, "You got a fish on that pole—pull it out!" So I finally decided I wasn't going fishing with him anymore. I am so glad that child abuse laws weren't in effect back then because if they had been, Daddy would have stayed in jail.

As I think back on Daddy, I can safely say that he was a smooth operator—at least he thought he was, but I had really found him out. Daddy delivered ice and coal to the country and some parts of the city. I watched him and noticed that there were some houses that he delivered to that he spent more time at than others. He would tell me to stay in the truck and not get out while he was there. Later he would come out with a smile of satisfaction, and I would turn my head as if I didn't see him.

There were times when Momma would go to Chicago to visit her sisters and leave us with Daddy, who would be like a rat when the cat's not home. He had just about figured out when Momma would check in, and he made it his business to be at home when she called. As soon as the conversation was over, he would make his run. There were times when she called and he was gone; to cover himself, he would tell us to tell her he had gone to the store. If Momma only knew.

When Daddy's health began to fail him, Momma had to drive him around. He found so many faults with her driving. He complained that she drove too close to the center lines, and when she got close to the edge, he complained that all the nails and glass on the road were always at the edge and she was going to mess up a tire driving that way. Momma kept driving, and Daddy kept complaining.

Back in those days it seemed that every time a car door slammed, one of us would scream, "My hand! My hand is in the door!" And Daddy would start cursing and say, "Keep your hands out the way!"

Chapter 9

The Narrow Path that Led to Town

There was a path that people traveled from the other side of the town, and it passed almost right under our front door. It was the path that led to town, and it was well traveled. Sometimes in the late hours we heard people going to and fro; sometimes they would be drunk—falling down and cursing—but they made it to where they were going.

One day a man who looked like an old Indian came traveling down that path. Daddy made friends with the man immediately and offered him a place to stay for a while. Momma was really upset at Daddy's decision and so were my brothers and sisters, but we couldn't voice our opinions. Daddy went and bought the old man a bed and put it in our room. Naturally we were very uncomfortable with his choice, but again we couldn't speak our minds.

Early one hot summer morning, as my brothers and I began to get out of bed as quietly as we could so as not to disturb the old man, we noticed that ants were crawling from his nose and mouth. You can imagine what happened next—we all tried to get out the bedroom door at the same time. Momma and Daddy ran into the room to see what our problem was, and yes, it turned out the old man was dead.

None of us could sleep in that room for a long time. Instead we slept on a pallet at the foot of Momma's bed. When we finally began to sleep in our own room again, we were still afraid. We would sleep with our heads covered, but as the months passed, we finally adjusted to it.

Chapter 10

Our Time Out with Daddy

During the summer months, when we were out of school, we would go to the place where Daddy worked, an ice plant where they made huge blocks of ice. They ran the blocks through a saw to cut them into smaller blocks, and then Daddy would load them onto a truck and cover the ice with a canvas.

He made his rounds through the country where people were waiting for their ice. Some would buy a dollar's worth; some would buy fifty cents' worth. Refrigerators weren't available for the poor at that time, so they would place the ice in their iceboxes, which usually kept their ice frozen until Daddy came again.

The ice route was very exciting to me. I watched Daddy change gears on that old truck, and when he got to gates, he would have to stop the truck and get out and open them himself because I was too small to open them. Finally one day I got up enough nerve to tell Daddy that

I thought I could drive the truck through the gate. He said, "Tomorrow I will bring a pillow for you to sit on, and you can try driving the truck through the gates."

The next day was like Christmas to me; I was ready. When we made it to the first gate, he asked, "You ready?" And I said, "Yes, sir!" Daddy got out and opened the gate and stood way back out of the way. As I drove through, he had the biggest smile of satisfaction on his face, and from that time on, my job was driving through the gates.

Daddy decided one Sunday evening to let me drive the car as we headed out to the country. The road was dirt with a little gravel. It had rained the night before, so the road was muddy. I was doing well, and Daddy had a smile on his face. As I drove along, I approached a long clay hill, and Daddy said, "Give it some gas." I gave it gas, and as I started down the hill, I was still giving it gas. Daddy screamed, "Get off the gas and stop!" So I tried to stop, but the car began fishtailing and ended up sideways on the road before it stopped. Daddy told me to get out of the car and get in the back, and I told myself that my driving days were over. When Daddy had cooled off, he gave me a verbal driving lesson; and later he allowed me to drive that same road—only by that time it was dry.

Daddy never had any special skills or hobbies outside of going fishing every now and then. He just worked all the time, and he never seemed to truly enjoy himself. I don't remember Daddy or Momma ever going across the state line as we grew up. Finally, when we were older, we kids would take them places that they had never been before, and they truly enjoyed it.

Chapter 11

Our Weekend Outings

O ur grandparents lived on a farm as sharecroppers, and sometimes my brothers and I would spend the weekend with them. The man who owned the place that they lived on would not buy poison to kill boll weevils, so all of us who were too small to chop cotton or take water to the workers were given the job of picking boll weevils off the cotton. We would put them in a bottle or a can and keep them until the day was over, and we were paid five cents a bug. Sometimes we would go home with five dollars or more—and sometimes less—but it was always fun.

As the years passed, my two brothers and I began to get away from Daddy and started finding little jobs on our own around the neighborhood. Daddy had an old lawn mower that we would push around town, seeking yards to mow, and we were successful at it. Some of the yards we mowed had old scrap bicycles, and sometimes we would mow a yard just for the old bikes. Finally we had a pile of old bikes in our own yard, and we worked faithfully until each of us had a set of wheels to ride.

In our neighborhood I was known as the fastest runner in town; I met many to compete with, but I still remained the fastest. I was also the fastest on the bike, but again I had much competition.

My brothers and I had committed ourselves to helping a man mow his lawn and rake it early one summer morning. Daddy had sent my brother to town to get something when the man that we were to help came to our home, so Daddy told me to go find my brother. I jumped on my old bike that I had cobbled together from many pieces, not knowing that I had not hooked the brake up.

I sped down Campbell Street, which was all downhill, and I was traveling at a good clip by the time I got to Church Street. I needed to stop and turn left, but when I tried to stop, there were no brakes to be found. So I tried to lean the bike over to make the turn, but there was a 1954 Chevrolet right there; and—*wham!*—my head hit the car right over the front fender. The bike was knocked back and wrapped around a light pole.

There I was, lying in the street, unable to move or say anything. Soon a crowd had circled around me, and I could hear them talking. I later found out that the driver of the car was the sheriff's wife, and I could hear her sobbing and saying, "I have killed that boy." I could hear someone telling her, "No, you didn't. He ran into you." But she never stopped saying, "I killed him."

There was a moment there on the street that I was in great pain, and I rolled up into a ball. Then all of a sudden, the pain all stopped, and I relaxed. Somebody in the crowd said, "Call the coroner, and you might as well call the funeral home also." I was still trying to tell them that I wasn't dead, but I could not say a word. Finally I heard the sound of sirens coming. It was the police, and they began telling the people around me to move back and give me some air.

The coroner had made it by then as well. I felt his cold finger touch me and heard him ask the crowd, "Have you called his parents?" Somebody said, "We don't know who he is," and somebody else shouted back, "That's Sampson's boy." Then I heard them say, "Move back. The undertaker is here." I heard the door of his vehicle open. He took out his gurney and walked over and spoke to the crowd.

All of a sudden out of nowhere I heard someone say, "Here comes his daddy." I could hear Daddy's footsteps—*bam! bam! bam!*—as he hurried to where I lay. He bent over me, with his warm tears falling on my face, and with a demanding voice he said, "Son, wake up." And with his help I got up, and he carried me to the hospital with a bloody nose, busted lips, and a bloody head. In other words I was messed up. After the examination the doctor told me that I had fractured shoulders and a fractured skull. I had lost a few teeth, but I was alive and was going to be well. There was a word from heaven (but we won't get to that just yet).

Chapter 12

My School Years

School was good while I was in elementary, but after that everything went downhill. I seemed to have forgotten everything that I had learned and couldn't pick up what I had not learned in the first place. I started feeling like I had learned just enough to make it, so I dropped out. But lots of encouragement from Daddy got me back in school. I stayed another year and then dropped out again.

I complained to Daddy that some of my friends had cars and I had decided to find a job so I could buy a car of my own. He made arrangements to get me a car and then showed up with a car called a Willy—the ugliest car I'd ever seen. I refused to be seen in it, so he returned it and came back with a 1957 Buick, which at the time was *the* car. Everybody loved it. So back to school I went.

While clowning around one day, I tore up the

transmission in my car. As you might guess, Daddy was mad, and he said that that was the end of the line. So I dropped out of school again, and this time it was for good.

Back then there were no decent jobs available for young, uneducated people, and today that still applies. With no education comes no experience.

Chapter 13

My Wandering Years

I became a wanderer and ended up in Chicago. My aunt took me in, and things were going well for a few weeks. One day my aunt told me, "You need to find a job so you can help pay bills."

I began job hunting and finally found one on a produce delivery truck. I didn't like it, though, so I found another one, making miniature cars and trucks. I tried to quit within hours there, but the parking lot had a gate that was locked until quitting time, which meant that I had to stay there until the day was over. But after that first day I never went back. Finally I made enough money to go back home. When I returned there was no welcome mat laid out, nor were there yellow ribbons on any trees.

One day, while looking for another job, I heard about a bus taking workers to Florida to pick fruit. That would be my way out of poverty, I thought. I found the person who was transferring workers to Florida and signed up to go. When the day came to leave, I was on board, and when I arrived in Florida, I felt like I had landed in paradise. It was good until it was time to drag that long ladder from tree to tree; but I got better and better and even started liking the job.

One day around the middle of February 1968 we came in from the fields, and as I was relaxing, the campus mailman delivered a letter to me from Momma. The strange thing was that the letter was quite large, so I hurriedly opened it. There was another letter inside; it was from the Department of the Army. Upon opening it, I was greeted by these words: "You have been inducted into the armed forces." The letter went on to explain that I was to report to the examining department in Jackson, Mississippi, the eighth of March. I cried.

After a day of testing, shots, and orientation, I had passed the examination, and I was sent to Fort Benning, Georgia, for basic training.

Chapter 14

My Military Years

I had a hard time adjusting at the beginning of my tour of duty, but after a few months, the training got easier and easier. Finally basic training was over, and I was off to AIT, advance infantry training. Again I thought I had landed in paradise; I was sent to Fort Ord, California, which was a wonderful place. From Fort Ord I was sent to Germany, another place that I truly loved. My stay there was brief—only a year. While I was there I felt the need to at least get a GED. When I finally received it, I felt like I had walked down the aisle at Harvard to receive my diploma.

Germany was a very exciting place to be; it offered so much to a wondering mind. The food there was out of this world. And when I was there (and it still probably remains the same way), prostitution was legal—I mean, legal. It was just like going window shopping: you could choose the woman that you wanted and pay the forty marks, and she would be yours for a moment.

The only thing I found wrong with Germany was the temperature; it was a cold, cold place. In the barracks that we stayed in, we could set bottles of pop out on the window ledges, and if they stayed there for more than five minutes, they would be frozen. The snow was always waist high.

I got very comfortable in Germany and thought that I was living the life. But all of a sudden my comfort zone was disrupted when I received orders to go to Vietnam. At that point my life seemed over. I knew that most of my classmates who had already gone to Vietnam had been killed or injured. Reluctantly I went and did my tour of duty. I thank God that I am still here to tell the world that God is good.

Chapter 15

The Readjustment Years

There were years when it was hard to adjust to life. My group leader and my platoon leader had told me to reenlist because I would not survive in civilian life with all that I had been through. I told them I was going for it anyway. I did, and thanks be to God, I made it.

But I couldn't seem to find where I fit. I had been under authority for so long that I had told myself that I would never ever be under another man's command again. I quickly changed that, though, and said I would always be under the power of Almighty God. So the struggle went on for years. I tried to find employment; but each new job meant that I was to be under someone's command, so I couldn't stay. And so the search continued.

One day as I searched for employment I ran into a man, a carpenter, who seemed like an answer to my prayers. The man told me that he had plenty of work to do and that he would give me a job. His name was

Joseph Williams, and we got along well. We built and remodeled houses and just stayed busy. All of a sudden one day Joseph asked me what church I belonged to. I told him I didn't belong to any church. He looked at me and said, "You don't belong to any church? What is wrong with you?"

I stood there looking stupid, and the only excuse I could come up with was, "When I find someone that's right, then I will join a church; and when I get myself right, I will join a church." Joseph told me that I couldn't get myself right, and that only God was able to get me right. He invited me to come to his church, and I agreed to visit.

After going to the church for several Sundays, I felt comfortable and like it was the place for me to be. The name of the church was Second Baptist. The building was in bad shape, as it was actually two little buildings they had put together. The roof leaked when it rained, and the floors had decayed from the dripping water. When women wore their heels, they had to make sure that they walked along the center of the floor where the floor joist was or they would fall through.

As time passed and as fate would have it, I joined this church, although I never knew the reason for doing it then. I also encouraged my wife to join the church as well, and she agreed. Everybody from the church she was attending thought she was crazy to leave her church to join that run-down church, but they didn't change her mind. She stayed with me and is still there.

I was given the position of deacon after the church carefully examined me and saw that the Lord was with me. I zealously stepped into my new role. At this church the pastor had two sons who were ministers and also attended the church. I finally felt confident about voicing my opinion, and I did.

My opinion was that we could do better than the crumbling building we were in. The church decided that I was right, and so we soon found ourselves at the bank trying to obtain a loan to build a new church. Our loan request was granted, and we began laying the groundwork for the new building.

After a few weeks Joseph and I were on our way, building our new church. We finally had the building framed and the roof on, and we were getting ready to lay down the bricks. But after checking on our bank account, we discovered that our funds had been used up. The work had to stop, and it appeared that the members had lost interest in the new church buildings. The pastor was happy with what was already there, so he didn't encourage the members to do anything.

Joseph and I went out and found other work until we could get funds to begin the work on our church. After several months we had enough money to do some work on the building, but one day on our way to work on the church, God called me into the ministry. While in the middle of the street my soul caught on fire for the Lord. My pastor was informed, and he reluctantly set a date for me to preach my first sermon. When the day came I was truly ready. My first sermon was entitled "What in Hell Do You Want?" and oh, what a crowd!

I wanted to preach more; but as I said, the pastor had two sons, and he would always let them preach and not give me a chance. The money again ran out, and the work on the church stopped a second time. I really felt burdened because I very much wanted to see the church completed. I began to worry daily about the condition of the church.

Chapter 16

The Day That Started
Without Me

To begin this chapter I'd like to say, "If you pray, don't worry, and if you worry, don't pray."

As I said earlier I joined a church where the members seemed to be content with the condition of their dilapidated church building. Each day I worried about it, and I attribute my sickness to worry. My head began to hurt daily, and the pain began to get more severe. I went from doctor to doctor, and every one of them gave me a different diagnosis. I was taking medicine for many symptoms that I didn't have and was still getting worse and worse.

When things seemed to have gotten as bad as could be, I was scheduled for an EEG, MRI, and EKG at Tyler Holmes Hospital on May 8, 1984. But on the evening of May 7, I came home with a severe headache, and I took some medicine and lay down to wait until the medicine took effect. When I was feeling better, I went outside and washed the car and then filled it with gas. Later on that evening, I went to bed, not knowing that I would not wake up the next day.

May 8, 1984, was just a normal day for many people in our neighborhood, town, and state—but not for my wife and neighbors. For them it was a sad and frightening day. My wife tells me that she observed that I was still in bed that morning when I would normally be up; and not only was I still in bed, but I was lying in a very awkward way. I didn't respond when she called me, nor did I respond to her shaking and tugging at me to wake me up. By that time I am sure she was in a rage trying to dial 911 and feeling like it was taking forever for them to get there.

When the EMTs finally made it, my wife would not get out of the way so that they could do their job. I was told later that they finally told her to move out of the way and she reluctantly moved. Upon our arrival at Tyler Holmes Hospital, our family doctor was there. He told my wife and family that I was clinically dead, for I had no vital signs at all, but that he was going to send me to Jackson, Mississippi, which was over an hour away. I was loaded up and carried to Jackson. I am sure that my records were sent with me, and they might have read DOA at Tyler Holmes.

With no vital signs and no signs of life at the ER, the staff at Jackson made no special efforts to attend to me. I was placed in cold storage, I assume to await the undertakers. While I lay there in that cold, cold room, the

Lord touched me. I regained consciousness and realized where I was but didn't know why I was there. I began screaming for someone to come and get me out of there. Many were lying in the room with me, some with their faces covered with white sheets. Others had uncovered faces, and they all appeared to be looking up to heaven.

Someone heard my cries and rushed into the room and carried me out. The staff began working on me in another room, and I still didn't know what was going on. Finally someone told me that a blood vessel in my brain had burst and they were trying to stabilize me so they could do surgery. Day after day they tried to stabilize me. Finally, after going in and out of consciousness, I was stabilized, but while I had been unconscious, I had seen the most beautiful sight, something no one could ever imagine.

I saw a place that had a path that led to the top of a hill. Along the path there were trees with birds singing in them. There were all kinds of animals; there were lambs lying beside lions. There was a bright light over the hill, and you could hear a massive choir singing songs that I had never heard before. I was crawling with haste to get to the top of the hill so I could join in with the choir; but every time I got to a point where I could almost see over the hill I would regain consciousness and hear a voice saying, "Not yet." Then I would pass out again. Each time I would try to crawl back to the point where I had stopped before regaining consciousness; but I was always at the bottom of the hill, and the soft voice would say again, "Not yet."

Finally I was stable enough for surgery. The surgeon cut my head open from one side to the other and discovered that the communication vessel in my brain had burst. The operation was a success, and I started down the road to recovery. It was a long road, but the Lord was there all the way.

A few days ago I was talking to a lady about the experiences that I had gone through, and I observed that tears were beginning to form in her eyes. She started telling me of the near-death experience that her son had been through. She told me that she had been raised in San Francisco, California, she had had several children while there. Her baby son was ten years old when she decided that she needed a quiet life. She felt the need to get away from the gang-infested and drug-filled neighborhood that she lived in, not only for her sake but also for the sake of her family, so she moved to Mississippi. Her child had always been active while in California, always playing in the streets and riding skateboards and bicycles with no problems.

Just a month after she moved to Mississippi, on Halloween night, she received news of a tragic accident. Her son had been by a hit-and-run driver and thrown ten to fifteen feet in the air. When she arrived at the hospital, her child was in intensive care. The doctor told her that her son was so broken up that he would be paralyzed from his neck down and that he would never be able to speak. At that point she began praying and crying.

The child was placed in a full-body cast and was given a room. He remained in a coma for a month. His mother told me that one day, while she was sitting by his bedside, the child began to move his head from side to side. His eyes opened, and he looked at her. She was so overwhelmed that she began screaming for the nurses to come see what God had done.

While they stood there the child kept nodding his head toward the window. His mother asked him what was with the matter, but he did not reply. She finally asked him if he wanted the blinds open, and he managed to nod yes. "Oh my God!" she exclaimed as soon as she opened the window. A bright light shone directly on the child. His bed began to slowly rock in a loving, soft way, and a smile came upon the child's face.

An old lady, whom no one had ever seen before, emerged from some unknown place and walked into the room. She said, "Don't be afraid, for the Lord is at work." After some minutes had passed, the child said, "I want some water." His mother cried out with such joy, "Somebody bring my baby some water," and water came from everywhere.

After a month the child was released, still in a full-body cast. As his pastor and the nurses were taking him to the car, they somehow turned his wheelchair over and couldn't get him up because of the weight of the cast. But with the help of the whole emergency room staff, they got him up.

After six months the cast was removed and he was given therapy for a month. The child was on his own after that. Today the child that the doctors had given no hope is a productive man with a family—all because of God.

Chapter 17

My Long Road to Recovery

The road to recovery was a long one. I gradually regained equilibrium and was able to go to the bathroom by supporting myself with the walls. I had gotten strong enough to make it to the hallway and greet those passing to and fro.

On Friday, May 21, the doctor came by to do his regular calls, and he was truly impressed with my progress. He asked me to squeeze his hand and found that I had great strength in my hand. He told me that he was going to release me and I could go home on Saturday. My wife had gone home to take care of some things that demanded her attention, so I called her to tell her the good news. So there I was, trying to get out of bed, as my plan was to have all my things together when she returned to the hospital. But I was paralyzed; I couldn't get up.

I was still lying there when she made it back. She

was really concerned that I was still lying in bed after the Doctor had released me, so I broke the bad news to her that I couldn't get up. I encouraged her to help me get into a wheelchair and asked her not to tell anyone that I couldn't stand, and she was obedient.

Home was a hundred miles away, but it really didn't matter just as long as I was going home. We arrived, and my brother-in-law made the task of unloading easy. I was brought in, and then I decided that I wanted to get into the bathtub. And with assistance I was able to get in and out of the tub.

While lying in bed I threw myself a pity party because some whom I expected to come see me never did. But some folks whom I felt wouldn't come did come. I watched the cars go up and down the road, but lying there as I was, I felt less than a man. So I began to pray and pray, and the Lord heard and answered my pray. On the third day of bed rest, I got up, went outside, got the lawnmower, and began mowing. From out of nowhere I heard someone screaming, "Get off that mower!" So I did.

Day after day I was getting stronger and stronger. Although I still had stitches across my head where I had surgery, I still felt the need to go.

One morning when I got up I decided to go and work on our church, which was still only a skeleton. I was met with resistance, but I told the protestors that I was doing a great work. And just like Nehemiah, I couldn't stop, for the Lord had brought me too far to stop. I continued to work until the church was complete.

Chapter 18

The Years of Adulthood

Back in the early seventies, I was alone and bored, and I realized that I needed a wife in my life. My sisters saw my look of sadness and began acting as matchmakers for me. One day they called me and asked me to meet them because they had found me a wife.

I hurried to meet them and, when I arrived, saw one of the most attractive, beautiful ladies that I had ever seen. I never dreamed that she would soon be the lady whom I would spend the rest of my life with. Although I had seen her on many occasions before that day, I never knew that one day we would say I do. She was—and still is—the lady of my life, and I truly love her. We have been blessed with three children and nine grandchildren.

I must admit that every day with her has not been a stroll in the park, and there have been days that I wanted to just give up on the thing called marriage and live the life of a bachelor for the rest of my days. But I am still holding on.

I finally realized what my hobbies were, and I truly enjoy what I have chosen. First of all I love fishing and fishing and fishing. I fish every season of the year, spring, summer, fall, and winter. Winter is my favorite time to get my boat and head for the river or some of my chosen lakes.

My next best hobby is woodworking. I have learned to build anything that is made of wood, and I truly enjoy it. After woodworking, I enjoy treasure hunting. I purchased a metal detector a few years ago, and I have been fortunate to have found many coins. Some are valuable, and some are not so valuable; but still I love digging in the ground and finding coins.

I also love gardening. Each year I try my hand at raising a garden, and so far I have done very well.

It has always been my desire to be the best father to my children and the best husband to my wife that I could be, but somehow that didn't turn out. I was blessed with one son, a stepson, and a step-daughter. I thought I was doing all the right things, but it turned out that they were all the wrong things. It became very apparent that the closer I tried to get to my son, the farther he got from me; but I have always been there for him and will always be there for him in the future. Whenever I see his number on my cell phone, I know he wants something, for he never says anything to me until he wants something. But I will always be available for him even though he ignores me.

As I draw near the end of this book, I pray that

my readers will be as inspired as I was in writing it. Although I have become a senior citizen by the grace of God, I am truly grateful to God for my ups and all of my downs. I can truly say that in this life there will be some pain, some disappointment, and some discouragement. I can attest to the words of the song that says, "I have had some good days and some bad days. But when I look around and think things over, all of my good days outweigh my bad days. Then I say, 'Thank you, Lord.'"

So today life might be filled with despair and agony, but just hold on. There is a bright side somewhere, and the darkest hour is just before dawn. So it's *not yet*. You're next in line for a blessing. Sometimes down in the valley of decision, you will find there are many others there, who don't know which way to turn. But the Lord left a remedy when he said, "In all thy ways acknowledge him, and he will direct thy paths."

I sometimes sit and wonder why life sometimes seems so hard to bear, but then I think about the word of God that says that in order to follow him we must suffer sometimes. The word of God also states that we must take up our crosses and follow him—even if it bears down so heavily at times.

I have made many mistakes in life just as everyone else has, and I am aware of the fact that we reap what we have sown. Although you might be sowing good seed now, there may still be some bad seed sprouting up that you planted years ago that you have not repented of.

The biggest problem that we face in this life is trying to understand others, and that's hard to do if you don't understand yourself. Often it's the man in the mirror that has a problem, so I've learned the hard way to get the mote out of my own eye first. I've learned to sweep around my own front door before I sweep around yours.

There are so many things that we don't yet understand, but we will understand them all in due season—just *not yet*.

I have always had a wondering mind and I had a wide imagination and I discovered that to imagine there must be a picture in your mind or to create something that we truly desire to see, to do or to be. I remember in my youth how I used to stand near the highway and watch 18 wheelers stop at the traffic light and I love to hear them change gears and I imagined one day I would drive one, my friends and I used to ride sticks for horses and I imagined one day be a cowboy, then I imagined a big dream house sitting on a hill, being the husband of a beautiful, loving and caring wife with 6 children, I also imagine one day having a few dollars in the bank and some of the things I imagine have come to be and the rest is in the layaway.

With all the things that I imagined I never imagined that one day I would get old and be concerned about my health and wellness, and I never imagine that there would come a time that I couldn't run as I used to, never imagined that my black hair would turn white, and that my footsteps would get as short as they have. Never thought I would see a time that we would have to wear masks and take shots to guard against a killer virus. Never dreamed that so much violence would enter into our world, When I was drafted into the military in 1968 gas prices was 34 cents a gallon and when I was discharged in 1970 it had jumped to 36 cents a gallon and I ever imagined that gas would be as high as it is today. There is another thing I never thought of and it is that all that we achieve in this life is useless and amount to nothing and it will be left behind, now that I have grown old I have a truly different imagination and that is being with the Lord in that beautiful place that he have prepared for us in that new heaven that he has prepared, one day we will be evicted from this old house that we live in and its so good when we are evicted that we have another house and its not made by hands but eternal and we will be with the Lord forever.